# Dear Cinderella

by Sue Graves and Holly Bushnell

**W**

FRANKLIN WATTS

LONDON•SYDNEY

Anastasia and Drizella were missing
their stepsister Cinderella.
They were sorry they had been unkind
to her. They decided to write her a letter.

3

The Castle,

Monday

Dear Cinderella,

We hope you like living in the palace.
We are sorry that we were unkind to you.
We are sorry that we made you
scrub floors and clean windows.
We are sorry that we made you
cook our dinners and mend our clothes.
Please will you forgive us?

From,

Anastasia
and Drizella

Cinderella wrote back to her stepsisters.

The Palace,
Tuesday

Dear Anastasia and Drizella,

Thank you for your letter.

You were very unkind to me.

You made me work too hard.

I was very unhappy and lonely.

My fairy godmother was my only friend.

I am glad you are sorry!

From,

Cinderella

The sisters wrote Cinderella
another letter.

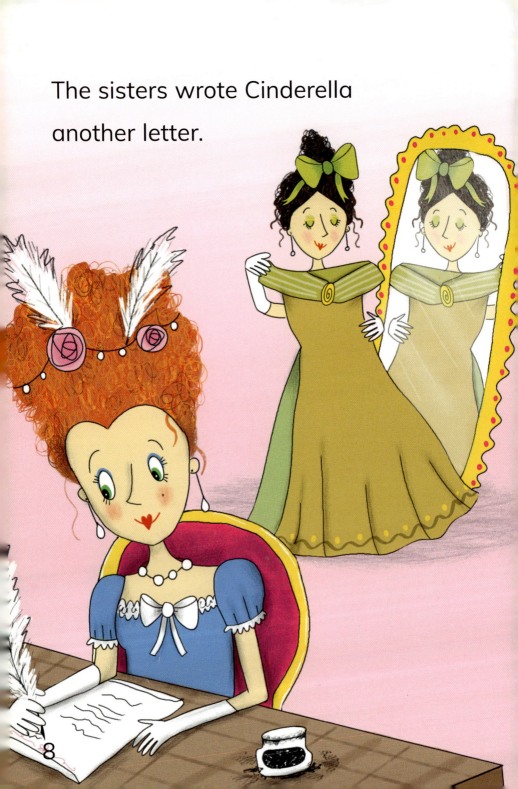

The Castle,

Wednesday

Dear Cinderella,

Thank you for your letter.
Drizella and I would love to come
to your wedding on Friday morning.
We have beautiful dresses to wear.
We promise to be very good and kind.
Please may we come?

From,

Anastasia and Drizella

Cinderella wrote back to her stepsisters.

The Palace,

*Thursday*

Dear Anastasia and Drizella,

Thank you for your letter.

No, you may not come to my wedding.

Only my fairy godmother is invited.

She was always kind to me.

You were not!

From,

Cinderella

The next day, the sisters wrote
to Cinderella again.

The Castle,

Friday

Dear Cinderella,

We were sad that you didn't invite us to your wedding. We went into the street this morning and watched as your coach went by. The crowd clapped and cheered, and we clapped and cheered, too.
You looked beautiful. We waved but we don't think you saw us.

From,

Anastasia
   and Drizella

13

Cinderella didn't reply, so the sisters wrote her another letter.

The Castle,

Saturday

Dear Cinderella,

We want to be friends with you.

We hope you will forgive us.

Please will you come to tea today?

We have baked lots of delicious cakes.

We have made a big red jelly, too.

We hope you will come.

From,

Anastasia and Drizella

The next day, the sisters wrote again to Cinderella.

The Castle,

Sunday

Dear Cinderella,

Thank you for coming to tea yesterday.

We hope you liked the cakes and jelly.

Please will you forgive us now?

We are very, very sorry.

From,

Anastasia and Drizella

Cinderella wrote back to the sisters.

The Palace

*Sunday*

Dear Anastasia and Drizella,

Thank you for inviting me to tea.

The cakes were *quite* nice.

The jelly was *quite* nice, too.

You must have worked *quite* hard.

But I will **not** forgive you.

I might forgive you one day,

but not yet!

From,

Cinderella

# Story order

Look at these 5 pictures and captions.
Put the pictures in the right order
to retell the story.

1

The stepsisters invited Cinderella to tea.

2

The stepsisters asked to go to the wedding.

**3**

Cinderella said she did not forgive them.

**4**

Cinderella said they could not go.

**5**

The stepsisters missed Cinderella.

# Independent Reading

This series is designed to provide an opportunity for your child to read on their own. These notes are written for you to help your child choose a book and to read it independently.

In school, your child's teacher will often be using reading books which have been banded to support the process of learning to read. Use the book band colour your child is reading in school to help you make a good choice. *Dear Cinderella* is a good choice for children reading at Gold Band in their classroom to read independently. The aim of independent reading is to read this book with ease, so that your child enjoys the story and relates it to their own experiences.

## About the book

Cinderella's stepsisters are feeling sorry that they behaved so badly towards her. They decide to write and say sorry. But Cinderella isn't ready to forgive them quite yet!

## Before reading

Help your child to learn how to make good choices by asking: "Why did you choose this book? Why do you think you will enjoy it?" Look at the cover together and ask: "What do you think the story will be about?" Support your child to think of what they already know about the story context and remind them of the story *Cinderella*. Read the title aloud and ask: "Who do you think will be telling this story? How will the story be told?" Remind your child that they can try to sound out the letters to make a word if they get stuck. Decide together whether your child will read the story independently or read it aloud to you.

## During reading

If reading aloud, support your child if they hesitate or ask for help by telling them the word. Remind your child of what they know and what they can do independently. If reading to themselves, remind your child that they can come and ask for your help if stuck.

## After reading

Support comprehension by asking your child to tell you about the story. Use the story order puzzle to encourage your child to retell the story in the right sequence, in their own words. The correct sequence can be found on the next page.
Give your child a chance to respond to the story: "Did you have a favourite part? Did you expect Cinderella to forgive her stepsisters?"
Help your child think about the messages in the book that go beyond the story and ask: "How do you think the stepsisters changed in the story? Do you think Cinderella is right not to forgive them straight away?"

## Extending learning

Think about the story with your child, and make comparisons with the story Cinderella. Help your child understand the story structure by using the same story context and adding different elements. "Let's make up a new story about someone writing to Cinderella. Who is it, and what happens in your story?"
In the classroom, your child's teacher may be looking at writing letters. Take the opportunity to look at the layout of a letter, for example, where the address and date are written. Find the question marks and ask your child to practise the expression they use for asking questions.

Franklin Watts
First published in Great Britain in 2024
by Hodder and Stoughton
Copyright © Hodder and Stoughton, Ltd
All rights reserved.

Series Editors: Jackie Hamley and Melanie Palmer
Series Advisors and Development Editors: Dr Sue Bodman and Glen Franklin
Series Designers: Cathryn Gilbert and Peter Scoulding

A CIP catalogue record for this book is
available from the British Library.

ISBN 978 1 4451 9103 4 (hbk)
ISBN 978 1 4451 9105 8 (pbk)
ISBN 978 1 4451 9104 1 (ebook)


Printed in China

Franklin Watts
An imprint of
Hachette Children's Group
Part of Hodder and Stoughton
Carmelite House
50 Victoria Embankment
London EC4Y 0DZ

An Hachette UK Company
www.hachette.co.uk

www.reading-champion.co.uk

Answers to Story order: 5, 2, 4, 1, 3